MILITARY SERVICE

CAREERS IN THE
U.S. AIR FORCE

MILITARY SERVICE

CAREERS IN THE
U.S. AIR FORCE

BY EDWARD F. DOLAN

Marshall Cavendish
Benchmark
New York

Special thanks to Captain Seth A. Henderson, instructor and unit admissions officer for Air Force ROTC Detachment 105 at the University of Colorado, for his review of the manuscript.

MARSHALL CAVENDISH BENCHMARK
99 WHITE PLAINS ROAD
TARRYTOWN, NY 10591
www.marshallcavendish.us

Copyright © 2010 by Marshall Cavendish Corporation

All rights reserved. No part of this book may be reproduced or utilized in any form or by any means electronic or mechanical, including photocopying, recording, or by any information storage and retrieval system, without permission from the copyright holders.

All Internet sites were available and accurate when this book was sent to press.

Library of Congress Cataloging-in-Publication Data
Dolan, Edward F., 1924–
Careers in the U.S. Air Force / by Edward F. Dolan.
p. cm. — (Military service)
Includes bibliographical references and index.
Summary: "Discusses service in the U.S. Air Force, including training, educational benefits, and career opportunities"-Provided by publisher.
ISBN 978-0-7614-4205-9
1. United States. Air Force. 2. United States. Air Force—Vocational guidance I. Title.
UG633 .D615 2008VB259.D65 2008
358.40023'73—dc22
2008039820

EDITOR: Megan Comerford   PUBLISHER: Michelle Bisson
ART DIRECTOR: Anahid Hamparian   SERIES DESIGNER: Kristen Branch / Michael Nelson Design

Photo research by Candlepants Incorporated
Cover photo: U.S. Air Force

The photographs in this book are used by permission and through the courtesy of: U.S. Air Force: 2–3, 31, 32, 42; Master Sgt. Chris Vadnais, 7, 50–51; Staff Sgt. James L. Harper Jr., 10–11; Staff Sgt. Bennie J. Davis III, 13; Tech. Sgt. Robert J. Horstman, 15; Tech. Sgt. Larry A. Simmons, 18–19; Staff Sgt. Markus Maier, 21; Airman 1st Class Kenny Holston, 24–25; Senior Airman Stefanie Torres, 27; Staff Sgt Angelique Perez, 29; Mike Kaplan, 34; Airman Matthew R. Loken, 36–37; Master Sgt. Scott Wagers, 40–41, back cover; Capt. Aaron Burgstein, 45; Staff Sgt. Joshua Garcia, 47; Staff Sgt. Douglas C. Olsen, 53; Senior Airman Brian Ferguson, 54–55; Staff Sgt. Desiree N. Palacios, 59; Master Sgt. Kevin J. Gruenwald, 63; Airman 1st Class Jonathan Snyder, 68–69; Staff Sgt. Jennifer Lindsey, 71; Rich McFadden, 73.

Printed in Malaysia
1 3 5 6 4 2

CONTENTS

INTRODUCTION
AN AIR FORCE IS BORN — 6

ONE
THE AIRCRAFT — 10

TWO
JOINING THE AIR FORCE — 24

THREE
AIR FORCE SERVICE — 36

FOUR
ENLISTMENT AND TRAINING — 54

FIVE
SALARY AND BENEFITS — 68

ACRONYM GLOSSARY — 76
FURTHER INFORMATION — 77
INDEX — 78

INTRODUCTION

AN AIR FORCE IS BORN

The United States Air Force was established as an independent service within the U.S. armed forces in 1947 by the National Security Act. However, the history of a military air component dates to nearly a century earlier. During the Civil War, decades before the invention of the airplane, the Union army had a balloon corps to collect information on the movements of Confederate troops.

The first successful machine-powered manned flight took place in December 1903; the airplane stayed in the air a mere twelve seconds. The airplane's inventors, brothers Wilbur and Orville Wright, spent the next several years developing their invention and trying to obtain a contract for it. In 1908 they succeeded in selling their airplane to the U.S. Army's Aeronautical Division, which had been established as part of the Signal Corps in 1907.

The Army soon began testing the airplane's flight capabilities and experimenting with its use in reconnaissance. In 1910

SSgt James L. Harper Jr., an aerial combat photographer with the Air Force, took this self-portrait while flying a mission over New Orleans, Louisiana, with F-15 Eagles and F-22 Raptors. U.S. Air Force pilots are among the best-trained pilots in the world.

CAREERS IN THE U.S. AIR FORCE

the Army carried out the first simulated bomb drop with sandbags, and a year later an Army officer took the first reconnaissance photographs from a plane.

Airplanes were first used in combat during World War I. Pilots spied on enemy camps, fortifications, troop movements, and supply depots. By the time the United States entered the war in 1918, pilots were flinging handheld bombs at ground targets and assaulting each other with pistols, rifles, and hand grenades. The warring nations quickly realized the potential of aerial combat. Machine guns that could be synchronized to fire through whirling propellers were soon developed. Pilots became ever more adept at air combat; a pilot who succeeded in downing five enemy planes was called an ace. German pilot Manfred von Richthofen, Canadian William Bishop, and American pilot Edward Rickenbacker were all famous aces.

At the end of the war, many nations made an air force part of their military structure; among them were Britain (1918), Italy (1923), France (1928), and Germany (1935). In 1926 the Army Air Corps (AAC) was established as a separate command within the U.S. Army. At first, flying units were largely independent of the AAC—most were linked with ground commands—but in June 1941 they were combined into the U.S. Army Air Forces (AAF) and placed under the command of General Henry "Hap" Arnold. During World War II the AAF consisted of more than 2.5 million personnel—it was the largest such force in the world. In 1947 the AAF became a separate military branch, the U.S. Air Force.

AN AIR FORCE IS BORN

By the twenty-first century, the U.S. Air Force was the largest, most modern, and best-equipped air force in the world. In 2009 approximately 330,000 men and women were active-duty officers and enlisted personnel. The Air Force had nearly 5,800 aircraft, including supersonic fighters, long-range bombers, helicopters, and special operations aircraft, which were flown by approximately 12,000 pilots. An additional 68,000 men and women served in the Air Force Reserve and 107,000 in the Air National Guard (ANG).

This book is aimed primarily at young men and women who are thinking of joining the Air Force. One reader may want to spend time in uniform from a patriotic duty. Another might wish to serve to honor the memory of a loved one or friend killed or injured in action. One person may see the Air Force as a career. Another may see Air Force service as the first step on the road to a university degree or the source of the technical training needed for future civilian work. Still others may join for the oldest reason of all: the desire to meet new people and see faraway places.

Time spent in the Air Force, no matter how long, brings rewards. It provides training and a sense of discipline that will be useful in civilian life. The academic and practical experience communicated in a variety of technical, administrative, and service areas can help anyone become an asset in any walk of life. Former members of the military are increasingly sought by civilian employers.

The U.S. Air Force has quite a lot to offer.

ONE
THE AIRCRAFT

THE AIR FORCE IS RESPONSIBLE FOR military operations in the air and in space, but it takes more than just pilots to ensure the efficiency and success of the Air Force; in fact, less than 5 percent of Air Force personnel actually fly the planes. Nonetheless, aircraft are central to the Air Force's mission. It takes a large, capable force of men and women to operate and maintain those aircraft, keep aircraft and personnel performance records, and develop new flight technologies.

The aircraft used by the Air Force fall into eight categories: fighter/attack, bomber, transport, helicopter, trainer, special operations, tanker, and reconnaissance.

A KC-135 Stratotanker (*bottom right*) refuels an F-15 Eagle fighter. Stratotankers enable fighters to stay airborne for lengthy sorties.

WHAT'S IN A NAME?

The names of certain planes—such as the B-52 Bomber and the F-16 Fighter—are widely recognized by the public. Yet this familiarity is seldom accompanied by an understanding of how the planes get their names or what the numbers and letters mean. Since 1962 the Air Force, as stipulated by the Department of Defense, has used an alphanumeric system of identification that names the three most important components of aircraft. This system is called mission-design-series (MDS) designation. In the MDS system each category of aircraft (such as the bomber) has what is called a mission designation, which consists of a single letter or a combination of letters. It is the first part of an aircraft's MDS name.

- A   Ground-attack aircraft
- B   Bomber
- C   Cargo transport aircraft
- E   Special electronic mission aircraft
- F   Fighter
- T   Trainer

Other aerial vehicles also have letter designations:

- H   Helicopter
- Q   Unmanned aerial vehicle (UAV)
- V   Vertical takeoff and landing (VTOL) / Short takeoff and landing (STOL) aircraft

When an aircraft is used for a different purpose than the one originally intended, the modified mission designation is indicated by the addition of a letter to the left of the original mission letter. Letters indicating such a modification include the following:

- H   Search-and-rescue and medevac
- K   Tanker
- M   Multimission aircraft
- O   Observation aircraft
- R   Reconnaissance aircraft
- U   Utility aircraft
- V   VIP/Staff transport aircraft
- W   Weather reconnaissance aircraft

The B-2 Spirit is one of the most technologically advanced bombers. The low-observable, or stealth, technologies make the plane difficult for sophisticated defense systems to detect.

Mission designation letters are always followed by a dash. The design number is listed immediately to the right of the dash. The design number is followed by the series letter, which indicates various types or models of an aircraft. (For example, the most recent model of the B-52 Bomber in production was the B-52H.) The series letter for the first model is always A. Series letters are assigned alphabetically, however the letters I and O are not used since they might be confused with the numbers 1 and 0. All production aircraft end with a series letter; a reference to an aircraft without a series letter—such as F-16—is to the general type rather than to a specific plane.

Military planes sometimes acquire informal names, too, that are often more widely used than the formal military designation. The F-16 Fighting Falcon, the KC-135 Stratotanker, and the CV-22 Osprey are all examples of aircraft with military designations and popular names.

CAREERS IN THE U.S. AIR FORCE

FIGHTERS AND ATTACK CRAFT

The fighter is a fast, agile warplane designed to intercept and destroy airborne targets (other aircraft and missiles) and to provide support for ground troops. Four types of fighters were in service in 2009: the F-15 Eagle, the F-15E Strike Eagle, the F-16 Fighting Falcon, and the F-22 Raptor.

The F-15 first appeared in 1972 and has been modified several times. Since 2001 the Eagle has been used in combat operations in Afghanistan and in Iraq. As of 2009 there were a total of 522 between the active-duty Air Force and the Air National Guard.

The F-16C/D and the F-15E are dual-role fighters; they fly both air-to-air and air-to-ground missions. All three of these planes have flown thousands of sorties since the September 11, 2001, attacks. F-15Es have also been widely used, particularly in Afghanistan in 2007. The Air Force has 1,280 Fighting Falcons and 217 Strike Eagles on active duty.

The F-22 Raptor, a multirole fighter, is one of the newest additions to the Air Force's arsenal. It is capable of both air-to-air and air-to-ground missions and is more reliable and easily maintained than other fighters. With its sophisticated sensors, integrated avionics (that is, *avi*ation electr*onics*), and supercruise technology, it is the most advanced fighter in the world. The Raptor was approved in 2005 to replace the F-117 Nighthawk and, as of 2009, the Air Force had 91.

As the name suggests, attack craft, including the A-10

THE AIRCRAFT

Thunderbolt II and the AC-130H/U, are equipped for combat situations. They have excellent maneuverability and are heavily armed. In 2009 the Air Force had 367 Thunderbolts, 94 of which were modified for forward air control missions. The active-duty force also uses 25 side-firing AC-130H/U gunships for close air support, air interdiction against pre-planned targets, and force-protection missions including the defense of air bases and combat search and rescue.

The B-52 Stratofortress can carry approximately 70,000 pounds (31,500 kg) of ordnance, including bombs, mines, and missiles, making it an effective long-range bomber.

CAREERS IN THE U.S. AIR FORCE

BOMBERS

A bomber is a combat-ready plane used to bomb enemy targets. As of 2009 the Air Force was using three bombers: the B-52 Stratofortress, the B-1B Lancer, and the B-2 Spirit.

The B-52 Stratofortress is one of the most famous and durable aircraft in U.S. history. Introduced in the 1950s, it is a long-range bomber that is also used in aircrew training missions. There are eighty-five B-52Hs in the active-duty force and another nine in the Reserve.

The B-1B Lancer, also a long-range bomber, carries more bombs and weaponry than any other aircraft or unmanned weapons system. The Lancer's payload includes general-purpose and penetrating bombs, naval bombs, and cluster munitions. It flies with two weapons systems operators on board. As of 2009 sixty-five B-1Bs were in active service. Because of the B-1B's importance, the plane is expected to undergo modification and upgrading.

The B-2 Spirit employs stealth technology, which consists of design characteristics that make the plane virtually undetectable to typical radar installations and thus enable it to penetrate and bomb the most heavily defended target areas. The Air Force had twenty Spirits in active service and one in the testing phase in 2009.

TRANSPORT PLANES

The transport plane is one of the largest aircraft operated by the Air Force. Ten types of transports—also called cargo

THE AIRCRAFT

planes—are designed to carry personnel or cargo; two others are designed to provide in-flight refueling.

The C-130 Hercules is one of the U.S. military's most versatile planes; the Hercules can drop troops in combat areas and be used for weather reconnaissance, aeromedical evacuations, airlift-support flights, and disaster-relief missions. The C-130 is often used in conjunction with the C-17 Globemaster, the Air Force's largest transport plane, to deliver troops and equipment to bases all over the world. In 2009, 151 Hercules and 158 Globemasters were in active service. An additional 181 C-130s assigned to the Air National Guard are used to provide relief to areas that have suffered natural disasters and to aid the U.S. Forest Service in fighting fires.

The KC-135 Stratotanker and the KC-10 Extender are transports modified (indicated by the K) to refuel other aircraft in flight. Both transports are also equipped for other tasks, including aeromedical evacuations. In 2009 the active-duty Air Force, the Air National Guard, and the Air Force Reserve were using a total of 453 Stratotankers and 59 Extenders. The forty-year-old KC-135s are the oldest planes in the Air Force. They are scheduled to be replaced by the KC-X Advance Mobility aircraft in 2013.

Several specialized planes are also members of the Air Force's transport class. The VC-25, better known as Air Force One—an extensively modified Boeing 747 commercial jet—has the sole mission of safely transporting the president of the

CAREERS IN THE U.S. AIR FORCE

Crew members make sure all the C-130 Hercules transport planes at Little Rock (Arkansas) Air Force Base are ready for flight.

THE AIRCRAFT

United States. (The presidential fleet actually consists of two Air Force Ones.) Air Force One is equipped with advanced navigation and communication equipment, a conference room, and presidential quarters. Similar planes—the C-37A, the C-40B/C—are used to transport members of Congress and the cabinet, other high-ranking government officials, and senior military commanders.

HELICOPTERS

A helicopter is a rotary-wing aircraft that takes off and lands vertically. The Air Force operates three kinds of helicopters: the UH-1N Huey, the HH-60G Pave Hawk, and the J and M production models of the MH-53 Pave Low.

The UH-1N Huey is a light-lift utility helicopter. Search-and-rescue operations, the airlift of emergency and response teams, and landing support for space shuttles are among its primary missions. Hueys, which were developed in 1970, are capable of

CAREERS IN THE U.S. AIR FORCE

nighttime flight and can seat up to thirteen people. The Air Force has sixty-two active-duty Hueys.

The combat search-and-rescue HH-60G Pave Hawk flies day and night missions to recover personnel dropped or downed behind enemy lines (the Pave Hawk is a highly modified version of the Army's Black Hawk). It is also used to rescue victims of natural disasters. In all, 105 Pave Hawks are being used by the active-duty Air Force, the Air National Guard, and the Reserve.

The MH-53J/M Pave Low helicopters are the largest and most powerful in the Air Force arsenal. The Pave Low's sophisticated Doppler radar (which allows it to detect and follow variations in terrain) and integrated avionics make the J and M models the most technologically advanced Air Force helicopters. Pave Lows are used by special operations forces (SOF) to infiltrate, exfiltrate, and resupply. The active Air Force has twenty-two Pave Lows.

TRAINERS

Trainers, as the name suggests, are aircraft designed specifically for training purposes. The Air Force has four types of trainers: the T-6A, T-38, T-1A, and T-43A. The T-6A Texan II, a single-engine plane, is a primary (basic) trainer for both Air Force and Navy student pilots. A more sophisticated trainer, the high-altitude, supersonic T-38 Talon, is used for training advanced students because it performs well, is easy to operate and maintain, and has an excellent safety record.

THE AIRCRAFT

NASA astronauts also train on the T-38. Advanced students learning to fly airlift or tanker aircraft train on the T-1A Jayhawk. Another specialized trainer, the T-43A, has up-to-date navigation and communications equipment and is used to train navigators who are to serve on strategic and tactical aircraft.

SPECIAL OPERATIONS AIRCRAFT

Special operations aircraft are used in a wide variety of specialized missions. Unmanned, multimission, vertical takeoff

Three CV-22 Ospreys take off from Kirtland Air Force Base in New Mexico. The Air Force uses the Osprey for special operations. The craft is capable of hovering and vertical take-offs and landings.

CAREERS IN THE U.S. AIR FORCE

and landing (VTOL), and special electronic-equipped aircraft are all used for special operations.

The E-3 Sentry is an airborne warning and control system (AWACS) that provides accurate, real-time surveillance at any altitude and during any weather conditions. Information is relayed to the Joint Air Operations Center, which is utilized by the United States, members of the North Atlantic Treaty Organization (NATO), and other allied nations for the air defense of their countries. The Sentry has a rotating radar dome that employs an IFF subsystem (the initials stand for "identification friend or foe") to detect, identify, and track aircraft. The Air Force maintains thirty-three E-3s on active duty and, as of 2009, had a new model in the testing phase.

The E-4B is a highly specialized aircraft designed to serve as the National Airborne Operations Center in the event that ground centers are destroyed. The E-4B provides a command, control, and communications center for the president, the secretary of defense, and the chairman of the Joint Chiefs of Staff, among others. Four E-4Bs were in active service as of 2009.

The primary mission of the E-8C Joint Surveillance Target Attack Radar System (Joint STARS) is to support attack operations by providing ground surveillance to commanders on the ground and in the air. The E-8C is equipped with computer and radar systems that enable it to be a platform for battle-management, command-and-control,

THE AIRCRAFT

intelligence, surveillance, and reconnaissance functions. The Air Force had seventeen in operation in 2009.

The MQ-1 Predator is a remotely piloted aircraft—an unmanned aerial vehicle (UAV). It came into service in 2005. The Predator, which can stay airborne for more than twenty-four hours, conducts armed reconnaissance. Along with the remote pilot, two sensor operators man the Predator system, which consists of four sensor-equipped aircraft, a ground-control station, and a special satellite link. The system requires approximately fifty-five technicians to keep it in continuous operation. The MQ-1 is equipped with a Multispectral Targeting System (MTS), which enables the aircraft to wield two laser-guided Hellfire antitank missiles each. As of 2009, 110 Predators were in active service.

The CV-22 Osprey is a versatile addition to the Air Force's special operations aircraft. The Osprey combines the hover and VTOL capabilities of a helicopter with the long range and speed of a turboprop aircraft. Special operations forces—highly trained specialized units—use the Osprey on infiltration and resupply missions instead of using both fixed-wing and rotary-wing aircraft. The Air Force Osprey, which is based on the Marine Corps MV-22 Osprey, is modified to operate at low altitudes and in difficult weather; it has infrared, radar, and advanced avionics systems. Fifty CV-22s are scheduled for delivery by 2017.

TWO

JOINING THE
AIR FORCE

THERE ARE FIVE WAYS TO SERVE WITH THE U.S. Air Force: by enlisting in the active-duty Air Force, by joining the Air Force Reserve or the Air National Guard, by completing the Air Force Reserve Officers Training Corps program, or by graduating from the U.S. Air Force Academy in Colorado Springs, Colorado. Air Force Academy graduates and those who complete the AFROTC program enter the Air Force as second lieutenants. Men and women who want to serve in the Air Force must meet certain requirements:

- They must be a U.S. citizen or meet noncitizen requirements.
- They must be between the ages of seventeen and thirty-four; those who are seventeen need parental consent.

Airmen with the 723rd Air Mobility Squadron get ready to unload wounded military patients at Ramstein Air Base in Germany. In addition to transporting patients who need medical treatment, the 723rd also deliver supplies to support humanitarian missions.

CAREERS IN THE U.S. AIR FORCE

- They must be high school graduates or have a high school equivalency diploma.

Enlistees must also pass urinalysis tests for drug and alcohol abuse and must meet a variety of legal and medical standards.

ON ACTIVE DUTY WITH THE AIR FORCE

Enlistment in the active-duty Air Force requires a commitment of a four- to six-year tour of duty. The Air Force is an organization of 330,000 people that needs 30,000 to 35,000 new recruits each year to fill all its jobs.

Service in the Air Force begins with an instructional period called basic military training (BMT). Basic training, which lasts approximately six and a half weeks, introduces new recruits to military life and teaches them the importance of discipline and teamwork. It is followed by a period of technical training in the individual's career field specialty. Technical training includes both classroom study and hands-on training.

A person interested in making the Air Force a lifelong career may advance through the ranks. Advancement is accompanied by an increase in responsibility as well as an increase in pay. Retirement is possible after twenty years of service. For enlisted personnel, Air Force careers are made up of periods of enlistment. At the close of each enlistment period, an individual is free to return to civilian life or to reenlist or join a Reserve unit.

JOINING THE AIR FORCE

Airman 1st Class Jeremy Meyers, a crew chief with the 34th Fighter Squadron, signals to pilot Lt. Col. Kurt Gallegos as he prepares for flight. Gallegos is with the 419th Fighter Wing, a Reserve unit that began working with active-duty airmen in May 2007 as part of the Air Force's Total Force Integration initiative.

AIR FORCE RESERVE

The U.S. Air Force Reserve was founded on April 14, 1948, a year after the Air Force officially became a separate branch of the armed forces. As of 2009 the Reserve was a force of approximately 68,000 officers and enlisted personnel and more than 440 aircraft. Reserve units work side-by-side with active-duty personnel and perform about 20 percent of the Air Force's workload. Joint responsibilities include aircraft maintenance, aeromedical evacuations, global fighter support, and aerial firefighting. The Air Force

CAREERS IN THE U.S. AIR FORCE

Reserve is the only group in the Department of Defense responsible for aerial spraying and weather reconnaissance.

Reservists are part-time Air Force personnel; all reservists are expected to serve a minimum of one weekend a month in drill and work sessions and to participate in an annual two-week training period. During a local or national emergency, a Reserve unit may be called to active duty, at which time a reservist's pay increases to that of full-time equal-ranking member of the Air Force. Federal law stipulates that a reservist can be kept on active duty no longer than two years without authorization from Congress. Under most circumstances the law also requires the reservist's civilian employer to reinstate a returning reservist to the job he or she held at the time of the call to duty. The reservist must have notified his or her employer of the call to active duty and must return to work immediately.

AIR NATIONAL GUARD

The Air National Guard (ANG) consists of 88 flying units and 579 mission-support units; there are units based in all fifty states. Each unit is dedicated to protecting its home state in times of crisis and, when necessary, to defending the nation and its interests worldwide. Like the Army National Guard, the Air National Guard offers training opportunities to its 106,000 members in a variety of fields, including technology, communications, clerical work, health care, and engineering.

JOINING THE AIR FORCE

The dual mission—federal and state—of the Air National Guard defines its duties. On a federal level, the Air National Guard is responsible for national air defense and also provides nearly half of the Air Force's aeromedical evacuation, tactical airlift support, aerial refueling, and combat communications functions. According to state law, the Air National Guard units must protect life and property and preserve peace, order, and public safety.

Service with the Air National Guard is much like that with the Reserve. Members are expected to spend one weekend each month in drill and work sessions and to attend a

An A-10 Thunderbolt II makes a night landing at Al Asad Air Base, Iraq. Senior Airman Daniel Young, a Maryland Air National Guard crew chief, directs the craft.

CAREERS IN THE U.S. AIR FORCE

two-week-long training course every year. A member of the Air National Guard is paid a part-time salary; when his or her unit is called to active duty, the person's salary increases to that of a full-time member of the Air Force of the same rank. Active service is also restricted to two years under federal law, and a civilian employer must reinstate a returning active-duty guard to his or her job.

AIR FORCE RESERVE OFFICERS TRAINING CORPS

The Air Force Reserve Officers Training Corps (AFROTC) program, like Army and Navy ROTC programs, provides training and instruction in military problem-solving, strategic planning, and the basics of military leadership, discipline, teamwork, marksmanship, and planning to young men and women. A graduate of the program is commissioned as a second lieutenant in the Air Force and commits to a four-year period on active duty.

AFROTC programs are much the same in essentials from campus to campus. The program has three basic requirements: to wear the ROTC uniform once a week, to participate in unit drill instruction at least once a week, and to attend an Air Force service course each semester. In every other way the campus life of an AFROTC student is no different from that of his or her fellow students. An AFROTC cadet must complete a regular college course load and graduate with a bachelor's degree.

JOINING THE AIR FORCE

Students who enroll in any ROTC program can expect to receive military and practical training. These cadets from the University of Portland and Oregon State University volunteered to help with construction on a house for ABC's *Extreme Makeover: Home Edition*.

The AFROTC program offers students merit scholarships to pay for tuition, textbooks, and uniforms, along with a monthly stipend. There is a four-year scholarship program for high school students planning on participating in ROTC during college, as well as two- and three-year scholarships for college students and express scholarships for languages and other areas.

The AFROTC program commissions about 2,500 officers each year. After completing their active-duty requirements, the officers can pursue a career in the Air Force or join a Reserve or Air National Guard unit.

These four female pilots, members of the Women Airforce Service Pilots, or WASP, have been trained to fly B-17 Flying Fortresses. During World War II they ferried the bombers to and from air bases.

WOMEN IN THE AIR FORCE

Women have served in the armed forces throughout the nation's history. It was not until World War II, however, that women were organized into units with specific duties. Among the 350,000 women who served during World War II were the members of the Women Airforce Service Pilots (WASP), who flew newly manufactured war planes to duty posts throughout the world.

In 1948 women gained a permanent place in the nation's military forces when Congress passed the Women's Armed Services Integration Act, which codified the position of women in the military. Like men, they could hold regular military rank and enjoy the privileges that went with it. Limitations were placed on enlistment and promotion, however, and they were barred from combat duty.

Since the integration act, women in the Air Force have achieved further equality and prestige.

1968
The Air National Guard accepts its first female enlistees.

1970
The AFROTC opens its membership to women following test programs at Drake, Ohio State, East Carolina, and Auburn universities.

June 26, 1976
The Air Force Academy admits 157 women—the first female students in the academy's history.

May 28, 1980
Ninety-seven of the 157 women graduate; the female graduates make up just over 10 percent of the class.

Spring 1993
First Lieutenant Jeannie Flynn becomes the first woman to complete an advanced fighter aircraft combat training course.

1995
Lieutenant Colonel Eileen M. Collins becomes the first woman to pilot a space shuttle; Captain Martha McSally becomes the first female Air Force pilot to fly a combat mission into enemy territory over Iraq.

2008
Of the 1,266 students admitted to the Air Force Academy, 21 percent were women.

CAREERS IN THE U.S. AIR FORCE

U.S. AIR FORCE ACADEMY

The U.S. Air Force Academy (USAFA), in Colorado Springs, Colorado, is the youngest of the military academies. The first students entered the academy in 1955 at temporary facilities in Denver, Colorado, and moved to the current location in 1958. The following year, 207 men became the first class to graduate from the Air Force Academy. Approximately 4,000 men and women attend the academy each year. Most of its nearly 600 teachers are Air Force officers.

U.S. Air Force Academy Cadet 4th Class Samantha Hill is formally accepted into the cadet wing. Cadet 3rd Class Nicole Elliot attaches shoulder boards to Hill's uniform during the ceremony in Colorado Springs.

JOINING THE AIR FORCE

The academy offers four-year undergraduate programs. About half of the students earn degrees in science and engineering; the rest major in the social sciences and humanities. The development of the character, leadership abilities, and technical skills required for a successful career in military aviation is a major goal of the academy's curriculum.

Admission to the Air Force Academy is competitive. Those interested in attending must be nominated for admission by the vice president of the United States or a member of Congress. Like any other university, the academy requires an application, a personal statement, and letters of recommendation. Applicants are also required to take an entrance exam.

Academy students receive government funds for tuition, supplies, and board and are also paid half of a second lieutenant's salary. The Air Force Academy commissions approximately 1,000 second lieutenants each year. Graduates must serve on active duty for five years, after which they may decide to pursue a career with the active-duty Air Force, join a Reserve or Air National Guard unit, or return to civilian life.

THREE

AIR FORCE SERVICE

THE AIR FORCE REQUIRES THE INTELLIgence, skills, and untiring dedication of its men and women to keep its aircraft, bases, training facilities, work spaces, and living quarters in optimum operational order. The administrative structure of the Air Force consists of major commands and field operating agencies.

MAJOR COMMANDS

Major Command units in the Air Force have national and international responsibilities. Each one must organize, equip, train, and manage its own personnel and keep its aircraft and support equipment in top condition. There are nine major commands: Air Combat Command, Air Education and Training Command, Air Force Materiel Command, Air Force Space Command, Air Force

Airmen from the 720th Special Tactics Group jump out of a C-130 Hercules as part of a water-rescue exercise.

CAREERS IN THE U.S. AIR FORCE

Special Operations Command, Air Mobility Command, United States Air Forces in Europe, Pacific Air Forces, and Air Force Reserve Command. A tenth command, Air Force Cyber Command, was started in 2007 and is in its provisional stage.

AIR COMBAT COMMAND

Air Combat Command (ACC) is responsible for organizing, training, equipping, and maintaining combat-ready forces to respond to emergencies. It also provides communications and intelligence systems and conducts global operations to gather information. The command operates over 1,100 fighters, bombers, reconnaissance, battle-management, and electronic-combat aircraft. More than 96,000 active-duty personnel and civilians work for ACC, which is headquartered at Langley Air Force Base (AFB) in Virginia. In addition, Air Force Reserve and Air National Guard units are assigned to ACC and can be mobilized in an emergency situation, contributing 57,000 men and women and 859 aircraft to the command.

AIR EDUCATION AND TRAINING COMMAND

The mission of the Air Education and Training Command (AETC) is to provide Air Force personnel with basic military training and technical training in various fields. The command is headquartered at Randolph AFB, Texas, and also has bases in California and Mississippi.

AIR FORCE SERVICE

AIR FORCE MATERIEL COMMAND

The mission of the Air Force Materiel Command (AFMC) is to research, develop, test, and evaluate weapons systems and keep them ready for combat. The command is headquartered at Wright-Patterson AFB (Dayton, Ohio), where the Air Force Research Laboratory is located. AFMC also maintains eleven centers nationwide where equipment is reviewed, repaired, and replaced. As of 2009, AFMC employed 75,000 military and civilian personnel.

AIR FORCE SPACE COMMAND

The Air Force Space Command (AFSPC) was established in 1982 and is located at Peterson AFB in Colorado. Its primary mission is to provide space and missile capabilities to U.S. war-fighting commands. AFSPC has approximately 40,000 military and civilian workers and an additional 13,700 contract employees. The command also launches and operates a wide variety of communications satellites and the nation's early-warning system. One of the command's most important tasks is to oversee U.S. satellite and nuclear-tipped intercontinental ballistic missile (ICBM) launch facilities, which are located in California, Florida, North Dakota, and Wyoming. The Air Force has more than 450 ICBMs.

The Fourteenth and the Twentieth Air Forces are components of the AFSPC. The Fourteenth, based in California, trains, equips, and provides support forces to space missions.

CAREERS IN THE U.S. AIR FORCE

Space duty technician SSgt Cristina Kavanagh and space duty officer 1st Lt Tanya Frazier work in the Combat Operations Space Cell. They provide space-based theater ballistic warning to U.S. forces in Southwest Asia, run global positioning satellite predictions to ensure GPS accuracy, and give space support to combat search-and-rescue missions.

AIR FORCE SERVICE

The Wyoming-based Twentieth is responsible for the Air Force's ICBM systems.

AIR FORCE SPECIAL OPERATIONS COMMAND

The Air Force Special Operations Command (AFSOC), headquartered at Hurlburt Field, Florida, oversees the work of the Air Force's special operations forces (SOF). The air commandos are the backbone of the SOF; their personnel are divided into three groups: combat controllers, pararescuers, and special operations weathermen. These elite troops ordinarily work in cooperation with special operations units of the other military services, including Army Rangers, Army Special Forces, and Navy SEALs. According to Department of Defense policies, women cannot serve as air commandos.

Like the other military special forces, AFSOC is highly selective.

Eddie Rickenbacker joined the 94th Aero Pursuit Squadron during World War I. The 94th was nicknamed the "Hat in the Ring" squadron because of the insignia painted on its planes.

AMERICA'S ACE OF ACES

The history of military flight recounts the heroism of many memorable pilots. One of the most recognized and admired is Captain Edward "Eddie" Rickenbacker (1890–1973).

Eddie Rickenbacker first gained fame as a race car driver in the early 1900s. When the United States entered World War I (1917), Rickenbacker joined the Army. He traveled to France as a staff driver but soon applied for flying instruction and quickly won his wings. Within seven months he had shot down twenty-two German planes in aerial combat, along with four observation balloons (used for sighting enemy artillery). His combat success made him America's leading ace and earned him the command of the 94th Aero Pursuit Squadron. His official total of twenty-six combat victories, or kills, was higher than that credited to any other World War I ace.

During the interwar years Rickenbacker worked in the two areas in which he had earlier won fame. He became owner of the Indianapolis Speedway (1927–1941) and was also involved with several commercial aviation enterprises. He was one of the founders of Eastern Airlines (1938–1959) and served as the company's president and general manager from 1953 to 1963.

In World War II Rickenbacker served as an air base inspector. While traveling across the Pacific on an inspection tour in 1942, his plane crashed at sea. Staying afloat on rafts, he and six fellow passengers survived for twenty-four days before being rescued. Rickenbacker described this harrowing event in *Seven Came Through*, a book published in 1943.

In the final decades of his life, Rickenbacker was a noted public speaker and traveled extensively to promote aviation and discuss the future of aviation technology. He died of pneumonia in 1973 while on vacation in Switzerland with his wife.

CAREERS IN THE U.S. AIR FORCE

Combat control trainees, for example, undergo fifteen and a half weeks of air traffic control instruction, three weeks of parachute training, two and a half weeks of airbasic survival training, and fourteen weeks of combat-control school (a combat controller specializes in infiltrating hostile environments to establish an assault zone or direct air support).

AIR MOBILITY COMMAND

The Air Mobility Command (AMC) provides three major services: aerial refueling, air evacuations, and airlift operations. Evacuations and airlifts entail the insertion of commando troops into enemy territory and their later removal, the rescue of ground troops or downed flight crews, and the delivery of food and medical supplies to victims of natural disasters. AMC is based at Scott AFB in Illinois.

UNITED STATES AIR FORCES IN EUROPE

The U.S. Air Force has been a presence in Europe since World War II. The United States Air Forces in Europe (USAFE), a command headquartered at Ramstein Air Base in Germany, maintains five main operating bases and fourteen secondary and support operations; USAFE employs more than 42,000 active-duty, Reserve, and civilian personnel.

USAFE's main operating facilities are located at the Royal Air Force bases at Lakenheath and Mildenhall in England, the Spangdahlem and Ramstein bases in Germany, and the Aviano base in Italy. The secondary and support

AIR FORCE SERVICE

Co-pilot Maj Ed Stack (*left*), navigator Maj Mark Parker, and loadmaster TSgt Karl Schramm are assigned to the 386th Expeditionary Airlift Squadron. The three men look out the window of their C-130 Hercules during a mission to Iraq.

operations—which are divided between air bases and air stations—are located in Belgium, Bosnia and Herzegovina, Cyprus, Germany, Hungary, Italy, Norway, Portugal, Spain, Turkey, and the United Kingdom.

PACIFIC AIR FORCES

The U.S. Air Force has maintained a presence in Asia since World War II. The area assigned to the Pacific Air Forces (PACAF) stretches from the west coast of the United States to the east coast of Africa and from the Arctic to Antarctica,

CAREERS IN THE U.S. AIR FORCE

an area covering forty-four countries. PACAF, headquartered at Hickam AFB, Hawaii, employs about 45,000 military and civilian personnel.

The command consists of four air forces: the Fifth (Japan), the Seventh (South Korea), the Eleventh (Alaska), and the Thirteenth (Hawaii). There are also nine wings (units), including two fighter wings and one airlift wing, stationed in Japan, South Korea, Alaska, Hawaii, and Guam.

FIELD OPERATING AGENCIES

The Air Force maintains thirty-four specialized field operating agencies (FOAs) that provide services, support, and information to Major Commands and other groups. There is a wide range of FOAs, which include the Medical Operations Agency, the Historical Research Agency, the Flight Standards Agency, the Office of Special Investigations, and the Security Forces Center.

AIR FORCE MEDICAL OPERATIONS AGENCY

The Air Force Medical Operations Agency (AFMOA), located at Bolling Air Force Base, in Washington, DC, develops medical service programs, policies, and plans. The agency's personnel, who work under the command of the Air Force surgeon general, conduct clinical investigations, supervise the management of radioactive material, and are responsible for aerospace medicine, health promotion, family advocacy, and bioenvironmental engineering.

AIR FORCE SERVICE

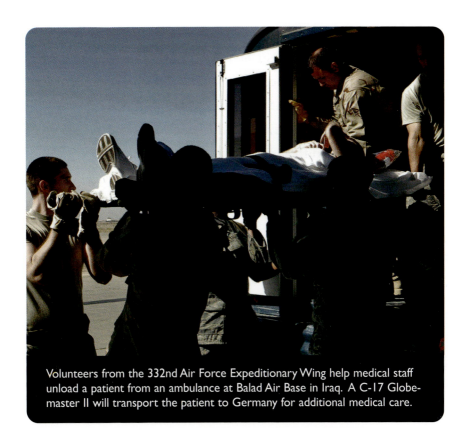

Volunteers from the 332nd Air Force Expeditionary Wing help medical staff unload a patient from an ambulance at Balad Air Base in Iraq. A C-17 Globemaster II will transport the patient to Germany for additional medical care.

AIR FORCE HISTORICAL RESEARCH AGENCY

The Air Force Historical Research Agency (AFHRA) is the repository for the Air Force's historical documents. Located at Maxwell-Gunter Air Force Base in Alabama, the agency provides research facilities for military students, faculty, and visiting scholars at Air University (located at the same base) as well as for the general public. The agency has a collection of more than 70 million U.S. military aviation documents, 90 percent of which are declassified.

CAREERS IN THE U.S. AIR FORCE

AIR FORCE FLIGHT STANDARDS AGENCY

The Air Force Flight Standards Agency (AFFSA) develops and certifies procedures, equipment, and standards for global flight operations. Among the agency's responsibilities are the inspection of airfields and of navigation and other systems. AFFSA, which is located at Andrews AFB in Maryland, is the lead command for air traffic control, landing systems, and airfield management.

AIR FORCE OFFICE OF
SPECIAL INVESTIGATIONS

The Office of Special Investigation (AFOSI) is the Air Force's major investigative service. The office's mission is to identify criminal, terrorist, and intelligence threats to the Air Force, the Department of Defense, and other government agencies, and to neutralize them. AFOSI is headquartered at Andrews AFB in Maryland and has 221 units worldwide.

AIR FORCE SECURITY FORCES CENTER

The Air Force Security Forces Center (AFSFC), headquartered at Lackland AFB in Texas, trains its staff to perform policing activities on an Air Force base, such as maintaining perimeter security and guarding base weapons and personnel. AFSFC is also responsible for training the dogs used by some Air Force law-enforcement teams.

AIR FORCE SERVICE

CAREER SPECIALTIES

All enlisted members of the Air Force specialize in one of four career categories: mechanical, electronics, administration, and general. After completing basic training, airmen begin their specialized training. The Air Force offers more than 150 specialized career paths, called Air Force specialty codes (AFSC).

Air Force specialty codes for enlisted personnel consist of five characters, both numbers and letters. The first character, a number, stands for the career group. There are nine in all: operations (1), maintenance and logistics (2), support (3), medical or dental (4), legal or chaplain (5), acquisition or finance (6), special investigation (7), special duty identifier (8), and reporting identifier (9). The career group number is followed by a letter designating the career field, and then a number designating the career field subdivision. The fourth character, a number, indicates the skill level: helper (1), apprentice (3), journeyman (5), craftsman (7), superintendent (9), or chief enlisted manager (0). A final number designates the individual's specialty within his or her career field subdivision. For example, an airman whose AFSC is 3P051 works in the support career group (3) in the security forces field (P) and the security subdivision (0) within that field; the airman has achieved journeyman status (5) and specializes in security (1).

Specialty Codes for officers are similar but have just four characters: a career group number (officers and enlisted personnel have the same nine groups); a number that desig-

CAREERS IN THE U.S. AIR FORCE

Majors Corey Simmons and Eric Von Trotha, both evaluator pilots, get ready to take off in a C-17 Globemaster III that is loaded with approximately 60,000 pounds (27,216 kg) of supplies. The joint task force mission is headed to Antarctica to deliver supplies to the National Science Foundation as part of Operation Deep Freeze.

AIR FORCE SERVICE

nates the utilization field; a letter designating the officer's functional area; and a number indicating the officer's qualification level. The qualification levels are numbered from 0 to 4 in the following order: qualified commander, entry, intermediate, qualified, and staff. The designation 2 (intermediate) is used only for pilots, bombers, and missile-launch officers; designation 4 (staff) simply indicates that the position is above the wing level—the second-highest level of command within the Air Force—and does not refer to the individual's specific qualifications. For AFSC 11A3, the officer is in the operational career group (1), in the utilization field of pilot (1), and in the functional area of airlift (A). The officer is qualified (3).

MECHANICAL CAREERS

Mechanical careers constitute one of the largest career paths in the Air Force. All things of a mechanical

CAREERS IN THE U.S. AIR FORCE

nature—whether aircraft or munitions or vehicles—require highly skilled mechanics to keep them in proper working order. In addition, warehouses, office buildings, gyms, and residential quarters also require mechanical maintenance. Some mechanics are specially trained to work on small intricate equipment, such as photographic gear, precision tools, and testing devices; others have been trained to inspect and maintain generators, air conditioners, air compressors, bomblifts, and other kinds of large equipment.

ELECTRONIC AND ELECTRICAL CAREERS

Skilled computer-system workers and electrical engineers are indispensable in ensuring the efficiency, accuracy, and effectiveness of Air Force missions. Enlisted personnel who enter electronic and electrical fields develop, install, and maintain radar systems, communications and computer systems, missile-guidance systems, navigation systems, and airborne and ground television equipment.

ADMINISTRATIVE CAREERS

An organization as large as the Air Force needs adept administrative workers to run its airfields and bases. Flights need to be scheduled, food needs to be purchased and prepared, facilities need to be built and repaired, and base police, fire, and chaplain services need to be supervised. Administration also encompasses accounting and finance. The men and women who fill these positions have an

AIR FORCE SERVICE

SSgt Sarah Hall, an aircraft maintenance craftsman with the 437th Aircraft Maintenance Squadron, is deployed with the 8th Expeditionary Air Mobility Squadron in Southwest Asia. Her job is to ensure that an aircraft is safe and fully operational; here she inspects fittings in the nose-wheel well of a C-17 Globemaster III.

important responsibility: to make sure that all Air Force personnel receive their salaries and benefits.

GENERAL CAREERS

General careers include those in intelligence, communications, air traffic control, the maintenance of biomedical equipment, diagnostic imaging, dental assistantships, and the supervision of the radar and surveillance systems that protect the nation from airborne attack. Although these careers are categorized as general, they require intense training and specialized skills.

ENLISTMENT AND TRAINING

ANY DECISION THAT WILL INVOLVE FOUR or more years of a person's life is a big one. The decision to join the Air Force is no exception. Some who choose to join are looking for a career, while others want to acquire skills for later civilian use, want to earn money for college, or simply want to do something that promises adventure and excitement. It can be helpful to talk with family, friends, and even a favorite teacher before reaching a final decision. Whatever the motive for joining, the first step is enlisting.

ENLISTMENT

Men and women interested in enlisting can begin the process at a local Air Force recruiting station. A recruiter can answer questions about the Air

Recruits in Flight 149 of the 322nd Training Squadron march to the immunization clinic. Even though it is winter, recruits are still expected to train outdoors and are given warm clothes and gloves.

CAREERS IN THE U.S. AIR FORCE

Force and military life and discuss career opportunities. He or she will also guide a new recruit through the enlistment process. Several documents are required:

1. Birth certificate
2. Social Security card
3. High school diploma and, if applicable, college transcript
4. A list of jobs held and places worked since age sixteen
5. Contact information for four personal references
6. A list of problems with the police, if any, including minor traffic violations
7. A list of places visited outside the United States
8. A list of places lived since age sixteen
9. A medical history, including a list of current medications

Noncitizens need to bring their permanent resident (green card) number and port of entry place and date.

The enlistee must next report to a local military entrance processing station (MEPS), where doctors conduct a complete physical examination and take a medical history. The Armed Services Vocational Aptitude Battery (ASVAB) is also administered here.

The ASVAB is not an intelligence (IQ) test; rather, it is a series of multiple-choice tests that are meant to identify an enlistee's skills and interests so that he or she can be placed in an appropriate job-training program. The subjects tested include general science, arithmetic reasoning, electronics, and mechanical comprehension. Recruiters can provide practice exams to help enlistees prepare for the ASVAB.

ENLISTMENT AND TRAINING

After the medical examination and ASVAB, enlistees sign a formal contract and attend a ceremony in which they take the oath of enlistment:

> I, _____, do solemnly swear (or affirm) that I will support and defend the Constitution of the United States against all enemies, foreign and domestic; that I will bear true faith and allegiance to the same; and that I will obey the orders of the President of the United States and the orders of the officers appointed over me, according to regulations and the Uniform Code of Military Justice.

The Air Force also offers a Delayed Entry Program (DEP), which allows an enlistee to wait up to a year before reporting for basic training and beginning active duty. People in this program attend the enlistment ceremony and then return to school, work, or family, business, or personal matters. However, they must report to duty with the Air Force at the agreed-upon time.

BASIC TRAINING

New Air Force recruits report to basic military training (BMT), conducted by the 737th Training Group, at Lackland AFB in San Antonio, Texas. More than 35,000 young men and women attend basic training each year.

At Lackland recruits are assigned to a training flight, an organizational unit of thirty to sixty trainees under the supervision of a training instructor (TI). Since basic training includes

CAREERS IN THE U.S. AIR FORCE

a rigorous fitness program that incorporates both strength-building and cardiovascular training, the Air Force encourages recruits to begin exercising prior to arriving at Lackland.

In November 2008 the Air Force implemented a new eight-and-a-half-week training curriculum. The aim of the longer and more extensive basic training is to better prepare airmen for combat situations and joint-service environments. Air Force leaders decided in 2006 that a revamped program was necessary due to increasing U.S. military operations. Not only are airmen being assigned to more varied operations than in the past, but many are being deployed shortly after technical training school, often to hostile areas.

PROCESSING WEEK

Recruits can expect to spend their first few days at Lackland undergoing immunizations and drug testing, getting haircuts, and training flight assignment. They will become acquainted with the Uniform Code of Military Justice and complete an initial physical fitness evaluation that includes sit-ups, push-ups, and a 1.5-mile (2.4 km) run.

WEEK ONE

During the first week of BMT, trainees are instructed in reporting and saluting procedures and practice basic drills. They are also issued identification cards and given medical and dental check-ups. Under the new training format, trainees are also issued weapons and learn how to take apart and

ENLISTMENT AND TRAINING

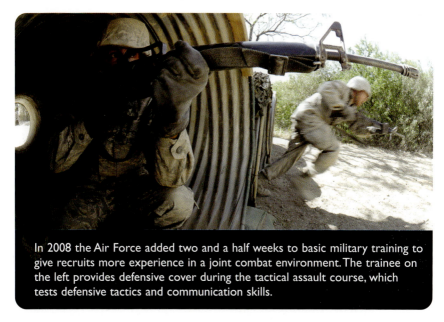

In 2008 the Air Force added two and a half weeks to basic military training to give recruits more experience in a joint combat environment. The trainee on the left provides defensive cover during the tactical assault course, which tests defensive tactics and communication skills.

reassemble their M16s. This allows trainees to become comfortable and familiar with their basic weapon before deployment exercises. Classes on nutrition and fitness, human relations, and the law of armed conflict are taught. Trainees begin daily hour-long workouts to increase strength and stamina; these sessions continue for the entire eight weeks.

WEEK TWO

Weapons cleaning and integrated defense are among the instruction given during the second week. Trainees meet with career guidance counselors to discuss post–basic training opportunities. They also undergo the first inspection of their dorms and their personal appearance (inspections continue for the remaining weeks).

CAREERS IN THE U.S. AIR FORCE

WEEK THREE

Trainees have job classification interviews in the third week of training. In accordance with the new curriculum, self aid and buddy care, which used to be taught toward in the field only at the end of basic training, is now taught early on in a classroom setting that is immediately followed by field application. The course covers basic first aid and advanced life-saving techniques, including how to use battlefield tools.

WEEK FOUR

Recruits participate in an obstacle course that tests their problem-solving skills. Chemical, biological, and nuclear defense training and improvised explosive device (IED) familiarization are part of week four, as is a course in antiterrorism.

WEEK FIVE

Much of the fifth week is focused on developing trainees' warrior skills so that they will be prepared for combat situations. Classes include those in the warrior role, joint warfare, basic leadership, security programs, mental preparation for combat, and basic situational awareness. In the field, trainees set up tents, participate in live-fire training, and practice hand-to-hand combat with pugil sticks.

One of the more significant changes to Air Force basic training is that it now mirrors the Air Expeditionary Force (AEF) cycle, which is the Air Force's approach to organizing, training, equipping, and deploying forces for emergency

ENLISTMENT AND TRAINING

operations. In accordance with this objective, trainees undergo simulated AEF pre-deployment preparation and assignment notification during the fifth week.

WEEK SIX

The culmination of basic training is the four-day Basic Expeditionary Airmen Skills Training (BEAST) exercise, which allows trainees to apply the training they've received during the first five weeks. The BEAST simulates the sights, sounds, and emotions airmen will experience in a deployment environment. Trainees must provide field security, use integrated fighting positions for protection, and perform tasks, such as convoy duty, during simulated attacks. The exercise also brings a realism to the self-aid and buddy-care skills.

WEEK SEVEN

During the seventh week of training, trainees take courses in combat stress recovery, financial management, environmental awareness, and career progression. They also learn about the history and organization of the Air Force and take ethics and sexual assault prevention classes.

WEEK EIGHT

In week eight, trainees must sit for a written exam that tests them on all the material covered during basic training. They are briefed on technical school, which all airmen will attend immediately after graduating from basic training. Trainees

CAREERS IN THE U.S. AIR FORCE

learn about the Air Force core values and participate in the 2.5-mile (4 km) Airman's Run. There is a parade and graduation ceremony, officially making the trainees airmen, at the end of the week to which family members are invited.

CAREER PREPARATION

All airmen who complete basic training are assigned to one of the Air Force's technical training centers for training in a specialized field. Centers are located at Kessler AFB (Biloxi, Mississippi) and at Sheppard, Goodfellow, and Lackland bases (Wichita Falls, San Angelo, and San Antonio, Texas, respectively).

At the technical training center airmen attend classes, participate in work groups, and work on independent projects under an instructor's supervision. There are periodic written and oral tests to track their progress.

The length of technical training generally lasts several months, though training in highly specialized areas may be longer. An airman is then assigned to a duty station and begins on-the-job training, a two-part program divided between independent study and supervised job performance.

Most enlisted personnel continue their education; the Air Force offers classes in areas ranging from leadership techniques to aircraft design and weaponry.

ENLISTED RANKS

As an airman gains experience and demonstrates increasing professional competence and leadership abilities, he or she will

ENLISTMENT AND TRAINING

These three crew chiefs are assigned to the 63rd Fighter Squadron. The squadron was stationed at Nellis Air Force Base in Nevada in support of the F-15 Eagle Weapons School Instructor Course. Senior Airman Michael Blankenship (*left*) fills out post-flight forms for an F-16 Fighting Falcon. Senior Airmen Gabriel Sheppard and Curtis Morgan change an argon bottle on an AIM-9 missile.

be promoted to a higher rank; promotion is accompanied by a pay increase. Each rank corresponds to a pay grade, or level, that is designated by an alphanumeric code. The nine Air Force pay grades for enlisted personnel begin with the letter E.

The four lowest ranks—Airman Basic, Airman, Airman First Class, and Senior Airman—are pay grades E-1 through E-4, respectively. An airman promoted to Staff Sergeant (E-5) is considered a noncommissioned officer (NCO). NCOs are

AIR FORCE RANK INSIGNIA

ENLISTED RANKS

Insignia indicating rank and pay grade are worn on the Air Force uniform sleeve (there are separate badges for each Air Force specialty). In the Air Force, rank insignia consist of different arrangements of stripes and stars.

Airman Basic (AB): no insignia

Airman (Amn)

Airman First Class (A1C)

Senior Airman (SrA)

Staff Sergeant (SSgt)

Technical Sergeant (TSgt)

Master Sergeant (MSgt)

Senior Master Sergeant (SMSgt)

Chief Master Sergeant (CMSgt)

Command Chief Master Sergeant (CCM)

Chief Master Sergeant of the Air Force (CMSAF)

OFFICERS

Air Force officer rank insignia are represented by gold and silver bars and leaves, an eagle, and silver stars.

CAREERS IN THE U.S. AIR FORCE

enlisted airmen who have been given command responsibilities. A commissioned officer usually has at least a college degree and has undergone special training; he or she delegates responsibility to NCOs.

Air Force NCOs also include Technical Sergeant (E-6) and Master Sergeant (E-7). The highest-ranking NCOs, those in pay grades E-8 and E-9, are Senior Master Sergeant (E-8), Chief Master Sergeant (E-9), and Command Chief Master Sergeant (E-9). These NCOs generally have at least fifteen years of service and are their commanders' senior advisers in matters concerning enlisted personnel. They may have several enlisted specialties and are usually experts in their technical fields. The Air Force does not have a separate First Sergeant rank; it is considered a duty, instead. A diamond above the star in the insignia denotes E-7, E-8, and E-9 NCOs that have first sergeant duties.

The highest noncommissioned rank is Chief Master Sergeant of the Air Force (E-9). At any given time there is only one. The duty of this senior NCO, who acts as the spokesperson for all enlisted personnel, is to assist and advise the Air Force's highest-ranking commissioned officers.

AIR FORCE OFFICERS

Most commissioned officers are graduates of one of the programs in the Air Force Officer Accession and Training Schools (AFOATS), an umbrella organization that includes the Air Force's ROTC program and Officer Training School

ENLISTMENT AND TRAINING

(OTS). An active-duty or Reserve airman who wishes to become an officer may apply to Officer Training School; courses are held at Air University at Maxwell AFB in Alabama. Applicants must have a college degree. The competitive program selects applicants for admission based on their aeronautical rating, specialty skills, character, leadership potential, community service, and academic accomplishments.

Officer Training School offers basic officer training and commissioned officer training. The basic officer training program is twelve weeks long; it is essentially a course in leadership that leads to a commission as a second lieutenant. Most graduates continue with training in a technical specialty.

The commissioned officer training course is five weeks long; active-duty, Reserve, and Air National Guard airmen are all eligible to apply. Airmen taking this course are commissioned prior to training and upon graduation are awarded a rank—usually between second lieutenant and lieutenant colonel—consistent with their professional credentials. The commissioned officer training course provides leadership training for judge advocates, chaplains, officers in the health professions, and medical scholarship recipients. After completing the program, all of these officers attend career specialty schools or continue their medical studies. (OTS also offers a Reserve commissioned officer training program, which runs for two weeks and is open to Reserve and ANG members only.)

Air Force officers are classified by pay grade; officer pay grades, ten in all, begin with the letter O.

SALARY AND BENEFITS

THERE ARE FINANCIAL, EDUCATIONAL, AND personal benefits available to members of the U.S. Air Force. The benefits for active-duty, Reserve, and Air National Guard members are slightly different.

BENEFITS

ENLISTED ACTIVE DUTY

1. Full-time salary
2. Thirty days paid vacation annually
3. Retirement income plus savings program
4. Free medical, dental, and hospital care (includes family members, if married)
5. Low-cost base exchange (BX) (department store) and commissary (grocery store) privileges
6. Low-cost life insurance

Airmen work on a plane as part of Red Flag–Alaska, a multi-platform coordinated combat operations exercise based out of Eielson Air Force Base. Spanish and Japanese forces also participated in the exercise.

CAREERS IN THE U.S. AIR FORCE

7. Extra income includes allowances for subsistence housing and uniforms

AIR FORCE RESERVE

1. Part-time salary
2. Full pay and allowance for meals and housing during the two-week annual training period
3. Health care for injury or illness during active duty or training periods
4. Low-cost life insurance
5. BX and commissary privileges
6. Retirement program

AIR NATIONAL GUARD

1. Part-time salary
2. BX and commissary privileges
3. Low-cost life insurance
4. State-specific benefits

SALARY, SPECIAL PAY, AND ENTITLEMENTS

An airman's salary depends on his or her rank and pay grade. Personnel in all the military services in a given pay grade receive the same base salary, which is fixed by federal law. Salary increases with each promotion and reflect increases in the cost of living allowance (COLA).

SALARY AND BENEFITS

Jessica Morquecho (*left*) and Melissa Palonio (*center*) of San Antonio, Texas, listen to recruiter MSgt Ruben Perez as he explains the Air Force's Delayed Entry Program.

Airmen may receive additional pay, however, for work involving extra duty, special skills, greater responsibilities, or hazardous working conditions. For example, parachute instructors receive extra compensation for the dangerous work they do. Furthermore, airmen may also receive entitlements (nontaxable compensation), usually for housing and clothing, depending on where they are stationed.

EDUCATIONAL BENEFITS

The Air Force, like the other military branches, provides airmen with the financial means and facilities to improve their

CAREERS IN THE U.S. AIR FORCE

lives and careers by continuing their education. The Air Force offers several educational and scholarship programs to its members.

MONTGOMERY GI BILL

The Montgomery GI Bill (MGIB) is a generously endowed government program that helps Air Force—and all U.S. military—personnel attain their educational goals.

Airmen on active duty, as well as certain members of the Reserve, are eligible to apply for this program, which is intended to finance a college education. The money can be used during or after active duty. To qualify, an airman must contribute $100 each month to the Montgomery program during his or her first year of service.

Reservists who want to take advantage of the Montgomery Bill must serve for six years and maintain a record of satisfactory drill attendance; those who do are eligible for up to thirty-six months of educational assistance.

COMMUNITY COLLEGE OF THE AIR FORCE

The Community College of the Air Force is a two-year instructional program designed exclusively for men and women enlisted in the Air Force. On successfully completing a program aimed at enhancing his or her career specialty, a graduate earns an associate's degree in applied science.

The college offers approximately seventy different programs; all students must complete courses in leadership,

SALARY AND BENEFITS

Capt Sam Allen, an instructor with the 563rd Flying Training Squadron, operates the controls of a battlespace simulator in a laboratory at Randolph Air Base in Texas. Allen is also the director of the Unmanned Aircraft Systems Fundamentals course, which will be used to train future UAV pilots.

management, and military studies. Men and women on active duty can earn credits toward their degree at either an Air Force advanced training school or a local college that offers the necessary courses.

TUITION ASSISTANCE

The Air Force reimburses up to 100 percent of tuition for airmen who work toward an undergraduate degree at an accredited college or university during their off-duty hours. It also provides up to 75 percent of tuition for graduate stu-

CAREERS IN THE U.S. AIR FORCE

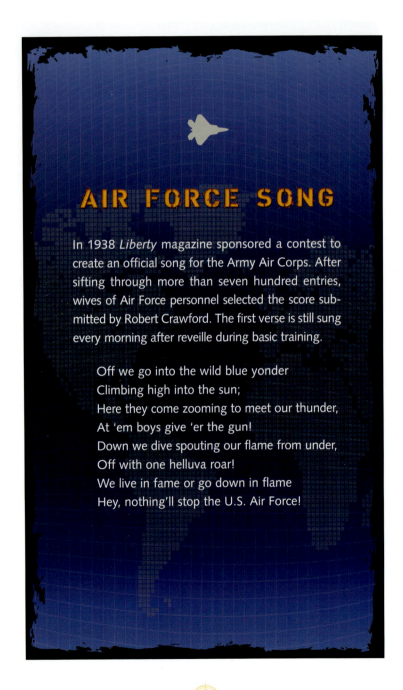

AIR FORCE SONG

In 1938 *Liberty* magazine sponsored a contest to create an official song for the Army Air Corps. After sifting through more than seven hundred entries, wives of Air Force personnel selected the score submitted by Robert Crawford. The first verse is still sung every morning after reveille during basic training.

> Off we go into the wild blue yonder
> Climbing high into the sun;
> Here they come zooming to meet our thunder,
> At 'em boys give 'er the gun!
> Down we dive spouting our flame from under,
> Off with one helluva roar!
> We live in fame or go down in flame
> Hey, nothing'll stop the U.S. Air Force!

SALARY AND BENEFITS

dents. Undergraduate and graduate degrees are beneficial to airmen pursuing either military or civilian careers.

EXTENSION COURSE PROGRAM

Air Force personnel also have access to the Extension Course Program (ECP), which provides a correspondence education in a broad range of both general and military subjects. Students progress at their own pace with guidance from instructors, who also grade their work. The Extension Course Program is free of charge.

BONUS PROGRAMS

The Air Force, like the other armed forces, offers bonuses for men and women who enlist or reenlist in critically needed career fields. Recruiting officers can provide information on the bonus program, bonus amounts, and areas in which specialists are most needed.

WHAT THE FUTURE HOLDS

Service in the U.S. Air Force, active duty or otherwise, can be a fascinating experience and lead to a satisfying career. Information on service in the Army, the Navy, the Marine Corps, and the Coast Guard is available in the other books in this series, which explain the nature, the requirements, and the opportunities that each branch offers.

ACRONYM GLOSSARY

ACC	Air Combat Command
AEF	Air Expeditionary Force
AETC	Air Education and Training Command
AFB	Air Force base
AFFSA	Air Force Flight Standards Agency
AFHRA	Air Force Historical Research Agency
AFMC	Air Force Materiel Command
AFMOA	Air Force Medical Operations Agency
AFOATS	Air Force Officer Accession Training School
AFOSI	Air Force Office of Special Investigations
AFROTC	Air Force Reserve Officers Training Corps
AFSC	Air Force specialty code
AFSFC	Air Force Security Forces Center
AFSOC	Air Force Special Operations Command
AFSPC	Air Force Space Command
AMC	Air Mobility Command
ANG	Air National Guard
ASVAB	Armed Services Vocational Aptitude Battery
BEAST	Basic Expeditionary Airman Skills Training
BMT	Basic military training
COLA	Cost of living allowance
DEP	Delayed Entry Program
E	Enlisted, in pay grade designation
FOA	Field operating agency
MEPS	Military entrance processing station
MGIB	Montgomery GI Bill
NCO	Noncommissioned officer
OTS	Officer Training School
PACAF	Pacific Air Forces
SOF	Special Operations Forces

UAV	Unmanned aerial vehicle
USAFA	United States Air Force Academy
USAFE	United States Air Forces in Europe
VTOL/STOL	Vertical takeoff and landing/short takeoff and landing
WASP	Women Airforce Service Pilots

FURTHER INFORMATION

WEBSITES

The official website of the U.S. Air Force
www.af.mil

The website of the U.S. Air Force Reserve
www.airforcereserve.com

The website of the U.S. Air Force for new and potential recruits
www.airforce.com

The website of the AFROTC program
www.afrotc.com

The website of the U.S. Air Force Academy
www.usafa.af.mil

SELECTED BIBLIOGRAPHY

Axelrod, Alan, and Charles Phillips. *Macmillan Dictionary of Military Biography.* New York: Macmillan, 1998.

Chambers, John Whiteclay, II, ed. *Oxford Companion to American Military History.* New York: Oxford University Press, 1999.

Holmes, Richard, ed. *Oxford Companion to Military History.* New York: Oxford University Press, 2001.

INDEX

Page numbers in **boldface** are illustrations, tables, and charts.

ace pilots, 8, **42**, 43
active-duty Air Force, 17, 24, 26–27, **27**, 30–31, 35, 44, 67, 72–73, 75
 aircraft in use, 14–17, 20, 22, 23
administrative careers, 49, 52–53
Air Combat Command, 36, 38
aircraft categories, 10, 14–23
Air Education and Training Command (AETC), 36, 38
Air Expeditionary Force (AEF), 60, 61
Air Force Cyber Command, 38
Air Force Flight Standards Agency (AFFSA), 46, 48
Air Force Historical Research Agency (AFHRA), 46, 47
Air Force Material Command (AFMC), 36, 39
Air Force Medical Operations Agency (AFMOA), 46
Air Force Office of Special Investigations (AFOSI), 46, 48
Air Force Officer Accession and Training Schools (AFOATS), 66
Air Force One, 17, 19
Air Force Reserve, 9, 16–17, 20, 24, 26–28, **27**, 31, 35, 38, 44, 67, 70, 72
Air Force Reserve Command, 38
Air Force Reserve Officers Training Corps (AFROTC) program, 24, 30–31, **31**, 33, 66, 67
Air Force Security Forces Center (AFSFC), 46, 48
Air Force Song, **74**
Air Force Space Command, 36, 39–41, **40**
Air Force Special Operations Command (AFSOC), 38, 41, 44

Air Force specialty codes (AFSC), 49, 51
Air Mobility Command (AMC), 38, 44
Air National Guard (ANG), 9, 14, 17, 20, 24, 28–31, **29**, 33, 35, 38, 67, 70
Air University, 47, 67
Allen, Sam, **73**
Andrews AFB, 48
Armed Services Vocational Aptitude Battery (ASVAB), 56
Army Air Corps (AAC), 8, **74**
Army Air Forces (AAF), 8
Arnold, Henry "Hap," 8
Al Asad Air Base, **29**
avionics systems, 14, 20, 23

Balad Air Base, **47**
balloon corps, 6, 43
Basic Expeditionary Airmen Skills Training (BEAST), 61
basic military training (BMT), 26, 49, **55**, 57–62, **59**
benefits, 68, 70
Bishop, William, 8
Blankenship, Michael, **63**
Bolling AFB, 46
bomber craft, 10–11, 12, **13**, **15**, 16, **32**, 38
bonus programs, 75

career paths, 49–53
cargo planes, 16–17
Civil War, 6
Collins, Eileen M., 33
Community College of the Air Force, 72–73
Crawford, Robert, **74**

Delayed Entry Program (DEP), 57, **71**

Department of Defense, 12, 28, 41, 48

educational programs, 30–31, 35,
   71–73, 75
Eielson AFB, **69**
electronics careers, 49, 52
Eleventh Air Force, 46
Elliot, Nicole, **34**
enlisted ranks, 62–63, 66
   benefits, 68, 70
   insignia, **64**
enlistment, 24, 26, 33, 54–57
   choices, 26, 49–53
   requirements, 56
entitlements, 71
Extension Course Program (ECP), 75

field operating agencies (FOAs), 36,
   46–48
Fifth Air Force, 46
fighter/attack craft, 10, **11**, 12, 14–15, 38
Flynn, Jeannie, 33
Fourteenth Air Force, 39
Frazier, Tanya, **40**

Gallegos, Kurt, **27**
general careers, 49, 53
Goodfellow AFB, 62

Hall, Sarah, **53**
Harper, James L. Jr., **7**
helicopters, 10, 12, 19–20, 23
Hickam AFB, 46
Hill, Samantha, **34**
Hurlburt Field, 41

insignia, Air Force rank, **64–65**
intercontinental ballistic missile
   (ICBM), 39, 41
Iraq, 14, **29**, 33, **45**, **47**

Kavanagh, Cristina, **40**
Kessler AFB, 62

Kirtland AFB, **21**

Lackland AFB, 48, 57, 58, 62
Langley AFB, 38
Little Rock AFB, **18**

Major Commands units, 36–41,
   44–46
Maxwell-Gunter AFB, 47, 67
McSally, Martha, 33
mechanical careers, 49, 51–52
Meyers, Jeremy, **27**
mission-design-series (MDS)
   system, 12–13
Montgomery GI Bill (MGIB), 72
Morgan, Curtis, **63**
Morquecho, Jessica, **71**

naming aircraft, 12–13
National Airborne Operations
   Center, 22
National Security Act, 6
Nellis AFB, **63**
noncommissioned officer (NCO),
   63, 66
North Atlantic Treaty Organization
   (NATO), 22

oath of enlistment, 57
officers, commissioned, 66–67
   rank insignia, **65**

Pacific Air Forces (PACAF), 38, 45–46
Palonio, Melissa, **71**
Parker, Mark, **45**
pay grades, 63, 67, 70
Perez, Ruben, **71**
Peterson AFB, 39
promotion, 33, 63

radar, 16, 20, 22, 23, 53
Ramstein Air Base, 25, 44

Randolph (AFB), 38, **73**
rank, 24, 26, 30, 33, 35, 70
 commissioned officer, **65**, 67
 enlisted, 62–63, **64**, 66
 insignia, **64–65**
reconnaissance aircraft, 10, 12, 38
requirements, 24, 26
retirement, 26
Rickenbacker, Eddie, 8, **42**, 43

salary, 28, 30, 35, 70
scholarships, 30–31, 72
Schramm, Karl, **45**
Scott AFB, 44
Seventh Air Force, 46
Sheppard, Gabriel, **63**
Sheppard AFB, 62
Signal Corps, 6
Simmons, Corey, **50**
space, military operations in, 10, 21, 33
special operations aircraft, 10, 12, 21, **21**
special operations forces (SOF), 20, 23, **37**, 41
special pay, 70–71
Stack, Ed, **45**
stealth technology, **13**, 16

tanker aircraft, 10, **11**, 12, 21
Thirteenth Air Force, 46
Total Force Integration, **27**
trainer aircraft, 10, 12, 20–21

training, **7**, 28–30, **31**, **37**, 38, 44, 66–67
 basic, 26, 49, **55**, 57–62, **59**
 specialized career paths, 49–53
 technical, 26, 62, 67
transport aircraft, 10, 12, 16–19, **18**, **25**
tuition assistance, 73, 75
Twentieth Air Force, 39, 41

U.S. Air Force Academy (USAFA), 24, 33, 34–35, **34**
United States Air Forces in Europe (USAFE), 38, 44–45
U.S. Army, 6, 8
unmanned systems, 16, 21–22, 23, **73**

von Richthofen, Manfred, 8
Von Trotha, Eric, **50**

wings (units), 46
women, 32–33
Women Airforce Service Pilots (WASP), 32, **32**
Women's Armed Services Integration Act, 33
World War I, 8, **42**, 43
World War II, 8, 32, **32**, 43, 44
Wright, Wilbur and Orville, 6
Wright-Patterson AFB, 39

Young, Daniel, **29**

ABOUT THE AUTHOR

EDWARD F. DOLAN is the author of more than 120 published nonfiction books. His most recent book for Marshall Cavendish Benchmark is *George Washington* in the series Presidents and Their Times. Mr. Dolan is a California native and currently resides near San Francisco.